Crisula Stefanescu

ON THE WINGS OF TIME

On the Wings of Time

© Crisula Stefanescu

English translation © Crisula Stefanescu and Monella Kaplan

Cover: Monella Kaplan

Published by eMotion Editions
An imprint of eMotion Entertainment LLC
United States of America
Email: editor@emotioneditions.com

ISBN: 979-8-9945524-0-7

First English edition
Printed in the United States of America

Crisula Stefanescu

ON THE WINGS OF TIME

eMotion
Editions

Author's Note

Several of these short poems were written in Romania many years ago, while I was awaiting departure for the West, in the hope that our family might be reunited.

Since at the time of departure it was forbidden to take anything handwritten other than a small address book with phone numbers, I entrusted to a friend a notebook containing poems and brief prose pieces from that period. It was lost and never recovered. As a result, apart from a handful of poems that I had the foresight to transcribe and send by post shortly before leaving the country, nothing of what I wrote in my early youth has been preserved.

Some poems written during that period, as well as others composed later in exile, were published in poetry volumes beginning in 1998, the year of my debut. Others, however, have never been made public. For this reason, I felt it might be worthwhile to gather them into a single book.

Reading the manuscript as a whole, I came to realize that these texts trace my existence in a seemingly random unfolding, where moments of joy and ecstasy, delight and happiness, alternate with moments of unease and uncertainty, of waiting and fear, much as they do, to varying degrees, in the life of each of us.

I now offer these poems to readers in the hope that they will recognize themselves in these miniatures, discovering states of mind they too have experienced throughout an often capricious existence: with its ascents and descents, its fragility and harshness, its fulfillments and disappointments, its certainties and mysteries, its fears and acts of courage, yet, in every case, shaped by that elusive and difficult-to-define feeling each of us calls *love.*

Editor's Note

This English edition of *On the Wings of Time* brings together poems written across several decades, originally composed in Romanian and later revisited in translation by me in collaboration with the author.

One of my intentions in preparing this volume was to introduce Crisula Stefanescu to English-speaking readers, preserving not only the meaning of her poems, but their rhythm, breath, and emotional temperature.

Each poem addresses a singular presence through the recurring invocation "My love," which functions less as a refrain than as a point of orientation — intimate, direct, and timeless. Read consecutively, the poems unfold as a sustained address, where love, absence, memory, and time circle one another without resolution.

Monella Kaplan
Editor, eMotion Editions

INVOCATION

My love,

it is enough to whisper your name,
and suddenly my words sound like song.

LETTERS

My love,

to shield myself from all that's wrong,
I write to you.
I write you letters every day,
and they are changing to poems
on their way.

Rite

My love,

I write as if within a rite.
I write, and words begin to mean
the more I write.
I write from a fevered need
to keep our present alive.

Verb

My love,

before a single verb
I bow down to the ground.
It is the verb *to love,*
a holy, timeless sound.

PERCEPTION

My love,

the dust thinks everything is dust,
the wind thinks everything is wind,
the stone thinks everything is stone.
Only I think you are everything.

DAWN

My love,

I am pure joy,
when filled with you,
I step from night to dawn,
drawn by diamond-sprinkled air,
white light reflecting
as if thousands and thousands of stars
were being born, then gone,
one by one.

GIFT

My love,

a woman is a divine gift to man.
And so am I to you.

ABSURDITY

My love,

to stop loving you?
To feed a vampire leaves?
To pass a camel through a needle's eye?
The very same thing!
To me — pure nonsense.
Yes, everything!

HARMONY

My love,

what a night!
Too small for our musical thighs,
moving in the harmony of a song,
the same tune, forever flowing on.

METAMORPHOSIS

My love,

as a cloud shattered by the wind
into smaller clouds
can never become again
the cloud it once was,
neither can I,
even if I wished,
be who I was
before I met you.

EMBRACE

My love,

hold me tightly in your arms,
as though I might vanish without them,
let me sip heaven from your lips
when I thirst for the lost paradise,
and let me feel my way to you
with the trembling gestures of the blind.

AUTUMN

My love,

autumn has dressed itself in gold
and anointed its skin with honey.
Is this the tremor before the Great Departure?
I, instead, have bared my arms
and wait, joyful, to blossom once more.

TIMEPLAY

My love,

lately I play with time —
I step lightly over days
and turn each night
into eternity.

DESTINY

My love,

I am bound to you
as gold to yellow,
as salt to its salty taste,
as the bird to wings
and fame to the praised tree.
I am bound to you like destiny,
unchangeable, meant to be.

HOPELESSNESS

My love,

never have I loved you more
than when I loved you without hope.

SHELTER

My love,

outside — tempest, a hurricane,
roof tiles dance on houses,
trees ripped from their roots
drift through strangers' yards.
Inside, afraid,
I move closer to you —
the only shelter left.

WINGS

My love,

your hands are soft wings, caring.
Why is it, then, that their warmth
makes me cold, trembling?

DANDELION

My love,

bow down over me
as you bend to gather from the grass
the fluffy flowers of the dandelion,
afraid that the moon,
slipping its ray,
might tempt them away.

FACES

My love,

my love has a thousand faces,
and I no longer know which one is mine;
somewhere among them I have lost myself.

RAINKISS

My love,

do you remember how we kissed
rain running loose from sky to night?
How we first forgot ourselves —
just for a fleeting breath —
and then forgot the world?
And called it right!

WILLOW

My love,

look at the tireless twisting
of the willow in the wind!
It feels like me, bound to the earth,
striving to reach you.

ECHO

My love,

what remains to me of a day
is the immense joy of being
and the fear that *today*
might not become more than a word
that others, after me, will speak.
A fragile echo they will keep.

STARLIGHT

My love,

it is a rustling night of silk,
the sky scattered with stars,
small islands of silence and light.
What a delight!

SHADOW

My love,

if you only knew
how vast your shadow grows in me,
until no space is left,
not even for who I used to be.
Our love is no longer a game
when everything steps inside —
yesterday, today, tomorrow,
happiness and sorrow,
side by side.

DREAMPATHS

My love,

last night I lost myself in a dream.
Two paths led me to you,
so hidden, so twisted,
that I stayed there until dawn, far away.

DISTANCE

My love,

you are so far away
that my thought can no longer hold you,
it only coils around you like mist.
Even memory's shadows tremble on my face,
afraid, it seems, of my own breath.
The distance between us,
written in every scar,
so far away you are, my love, so far!

CONSTELLATION

My love,

last night the stars felt close enough
to reach and take them all.
I didn't move, I just stood there,
spellbound, still,
under a sky that seemed to fall.

BLOSSOMS

My love,

the sky has covered itself
in apple and cherry blossoms.
Braiding blades of grass,
I wait for fruit to come,
and while I wait,
silence wraps me slowly
in its shade.

Reflection

My love,

today I ran into myself on the street,
caught my reflection
before we could meet.
I was coming at me,
no pause, no space,
moving through the noise,
wearing your face.

Labyrinth

My love,

I carved into your flesh
winding paths like through a labyrinth.
I want it without exits, sealed,
with no escape to send,
a maze that folds forever, without end.

NIGHTCROSSING

My love,

tomorrow feels a lifetime away.
To get there without you,
I have to cross one more night,
slow-burning, awake,
counting the dark I still have to take.

CROSSROADS

My love,

I stand at a crossroads,
losing direction,
as if I am only who I was
when both of us,
absent and alone,
passed one another,
unknown.

AFTERSTORM

My love,

didn't you know
that after a departure,
like after a storm,
whole worlds collapse,
and other worlds are born?

OVERGROWN

My love,

I once knew
a place of tall trees,
lost in thought.
Now grass has covered,
in gentle waves,
the paths of long ago
soft and slow.

CREATION

My love,

perhaps I am shaped of dust and clay,
yet kneaded by godly hands this way.

SPRINGS

My love,

exhausted springs don't die.
They pull back quietly, they hide,
slipping away from open sight.
For just a while, they turn inside,
to keep their strength, their secret light.

POPPIES

My love,

a field - a field of poppies bright!
A field of poppies drowned in light!
Through burning red, a single hue:
a murmur rising — only you.

SUMMER

My love,

autumn has set the forests on fire,
the sea regains its longed-for solitude,
the shadows of birds vanish
somewhere far away.
Only for us does summer stay.

ANGEL

My love,

last night an angel came to us to stay.
He spoke with passion of his fall away.

DANAE

My love,

locked within myself like Danaë
in her high tower,
I wait for you to come,
so I may bloom
beneath the falling light,
and my body,
entwined around yours,
learns to bear what flesh once bore
beneath the weight
of sacred rain
that falls on me again.

BEING

My love,

I desire *being* more than *having*.
If I wish to have anything,
love would be the only thing.

NOON

My love,

noon rests in silence,
warm and deep.
The fields breathe hush
before they sleep.
Warm scent drifts up
from earth and air,
dreams rise and swell —
we meet them there.
Warm skin, a shared delay,
desire learns to breathe today.

VINTAGE

My love,

the dizzying scent of ripened wine
rises slowly from scorched hills,
vine after vine,
while wild horses, digging deep,
lose themselves across my sleep.

ARRIVAL

My love,

you told me that love is just a journey
and in the end we find a place
where dreams may dwell forever.
I think I have arrived,
for every time you look at me,
I already feel at home.

NESTS

My love,

my hands fell asleep upon my knees,
two fragile nests for unborn dreams.

FALLEN

My love,

we were inseparable,
wing to wing,
no distance and no doubt,
one body held by everything.

Now each of us alone, silent, sad,
weary and distant,
like the wings of a bird
fallen from the heights.

BIRD

My love,

yesterday, I saw a bird that couldn't fly.
I cried.
Today, a thousand daring dreams have died.
I didn't even sigh.

FATE

My love,

there's nowhere fate cannot find,
no armor strong, no borrowed mind,
no name we wear to hide or flee,
from what will come — inevitably.

INFINITY

My love,

as countless as sand and river stone,
as stars, as leaves, as cruelty known —
so vast, so fierce, so true above
is all the measure of my love.

WHISPER

My love,

night thickens with unspoken signs.
The grass whispers.
A salamander sighs.

Which paths might you still wander
so I could meet you there
and feel your tender hand rest here
on my shoulder?

WINTER

My love,

days enter winter, stripped and bare.
The sea unravels into shell and algae air.
Above us, time's ash softly falls,
settling slow on crumbling walls.

PEARLS

My love,

inseparable as oyster shells,
we throb with all the shoreline tells
and, trembling through time's patient swirl,
give birth to giants — blush-bright pearls.

TEMPEST

My love,

what storm has broken loose tonight!
The harbor lost its final light.
Now night, gone mad, in kisses twines
with crazy wind and broken signs.

BUTTERFLY

My love,

I still do not know what I wish to be:
a bird that breaks toward open sky,
or butterfly from bloom to bloom,
in love with things that fade too soon.

SILENCE

My love,

where silence speaks,
words are excess.

TSUNAMI

My love,

our love is like a sea
stirred by a tsunami,
raging underneath,
that wipes away in just one breath
my years, my fears, my grief.

RELEASE

My love,

slowly,
I learned the cost of letting go.

NESTING

My love,

silence has nested between us —
a mute bird,
brooding its eggs of imagined guilt.
It shelters indifference,
forgetting's cold weight,
waiting to hatch its inevitable fate.

CIPHER

My love,

love is a secret code
spoken by two —
once ours, now lost.

BLOOM

My love,

in the blazing sun
I hear the grass sing praise
to the light as days pass.
My bones grow soft, take root,
and then, bud into flowers —
bloom again.

EVENING

My love,

in the evening I may be wiser
than in the morning now gone
yet not wise enough
for the night to come.

HOURGLASS

My love,

without you,
I'm a shattered hourglass,
the sand all run,
a clock with fallen hands
and rusted key,
a bird with a single wing,
that has forgotten how to sing.

RETURN

My love,

come back,
you'll never know how much I cried.
I will wait for you like Mona Lisa,
frozen in a smile,
while years drift by all the while.

HARP

My love,

do not take from me your heart —
the harp on which my angel once wept.
Do not take from me your body,
for without it, what remains of this life,
or of my soul's deep regret?

FRAGILITY

My love,

what more is there to say?
I'm just as invulnerable
as a soap-bubble blown away.

RECOGNITION

My love,

I knew you at first sight.
Only you believed
this was our first encounter.
We had met before,
in other lives,
or in a life gone long ago,
I was already yours, as evermore.

LONELINESS

My love,

I carry on my back
an invisible hump
of loneliness.

NOTHINGNESS

My love,

moths of nothingness
have gnawed at the garments of my soul,
mysterious as a concubine's.
Between you and me, silence —
a giant, ravenous worm.
The word demands a mad courage,
and once spoken
often resembles
a deep sword wound.

SLIPPING

My love,

I am the woman of sand.
Can't you feel
how I'm already slipping
through your fingers?

IMMORTALITY

My love,

only love stands above death;
only the Angel of Love
can face the Angel of the End.

I stretch my palm toward you
and rain keeps falling
into my open hand,
from which you will never drink.

DESERT

My love,

so much time has passed
since you left
that the desert
has reached me
and left on my lips
the taste of sand.

PASSION

My love,

the burning passion of the flesh
I wish to teach, slowly, to die,
yet I hesitate, uncertain,
one more day, one more evening,
lingering where desire won't say goodbye.

SUNBEAM

My love,

a ray of sunlight appears.
We warm ourselves by it
until we sprout like grains of wheat,
then torn by wind.

SUNRISE

My love,

the sun's blood-red eye
opens over the sea.
With you between my eyelids,
I shiver at the beauty being born,
that in my soul slips like vapor.
There is as much joy in the rising sun
as sorrow in the night now gone.

BLOOD

My love,

the blood once feverish
now carries the scent of green shadows,
flows slowly, pale and shallow.

RENEWAL

My love,

how can I make you love me anew?
Might a tear from my eyes
soften your heart?
Can a dried flower
bloom again in the rain?
Or only ache in pain?

SEA

My love,

our desire is a raging sea —
its roar covers everything.

TIME

My love,

do you know why time has wings?
It learned to soar
from the tender beat of our hearts,
to carry our dreams
through all its parts.

WISDOM

My love,

a wise man once said
that between good and evil
there is an unbridgeable chasm,
like the one between present and past.
I smiled at how it would last.

ABSENCE

My love,

do you know I grow old
on the nights you do not come?
Do you know
I whisper to the empty room?
Do you know
that even absence remembers you?
Do you know all of this?

VOID

My love,

how can I live without you?
Like learning
to live in my own absence.

SURRENDER

My love,

my life is a blank check
in your hands.
Write whatever you wish.

EPISTLES

My love,

I believe that in another life,
under the name Mariana Alcoforado,
I poured my heart into letters for you.

SNOW

My love,

snow falls in heavy flakes,
and spirals of smoke curl above the houses
rising like enormous life buoys
as if they could carry us
through the gray winter air.

CAW

My love,

yesterday,
I gazed dreamily out the window —
a harsh caw warned me
that dreaming is not innocent.

STRANGER

My love,

your face is hardened by storms.
Where do you come from?
And to which world,
unknown to me,
do you now belong?

NEST

My love,

under time's wing,
my soul, a fragile nest of fears,
shivering in the shadow of your absence.

INNOCENCE

My love,

above us, a sun softened by fog,
a dream before it takes shape,
innocent as a lamb
on its first morning,
as is my heart,
for you.

TRANSLATION

My love,

your words,
translated for me by ill-wishers —
a lying history,
that bends the shape of you and me.

BOND

My love,

between you and me,
a mysterious bond —
like that between statue and pedestal,
between river and shore,
between shadow and light,
between past and memory,
between twilight and eternity.

MIRRORING

My love,

the reflections of water double us,
our forms trembling together,
as dreams double life,
and my heart mirrors yours.

ORPHEUS

My love,

in the melody of your voice,
I drift to sleep —
like forest beasts
entranced by Orpheus' song.

CHAIN

My love,

life is made of moments,
as armor is made of links,
each one forged with you.

AWAITING

My love,

I have waited for you so long
that the old desk has grown roots,
your letters have sprouted,
and the front door slowly molds,
as the story of us slowly unfolds.

CLOUDS

My love,

harsh words cover our thoughts
as black clouds sometimes cover the sky.
But even the heaviest clouds will drift away,
and light appears again one day.

POSSESSION

My love,

with a single glance, rich in caress,
you take from my mind all I possess
and lay in my soul all you desire —
and yet,
I still wonder what you will take next.

FUJI

My love,

as ash never settles over Fuji,
so the ash of time
cannot settle over our love.

THRESHOLD

My love,

if you come to me,
as you promised,
at the gate of my home
a sign will read:
From here on,
time no longer passes.

PANTHER

My love,

sadness cannot be killed with an arrow.
A tamed panther waits behind bars
patient for its daily ration —
yet your hand can soothe its restlessness.

ROOTS

My love,

can one ever truly part from what has been?
Can a grown tree,
nourished for years by voluptuous soil,
be uprooted and planted elsewhere?
Yet our roots entwined will keep the love alive,
helping it endure and survive.

WINTERTREE

My love,

without you I am nothing more
than a naked tree in winter
clinging to the wind.

QUEST

My love,

the search for perfect love —
what a tempting path!
If only one did not lose the way,
perhaps my heart would choose to stay.

FERMENTATION

My love,

the must ferments in barrels
and lightly makes me dizzy,
as once your burning words did,
deepening my longing.

GARDEN

My love,

it is autumn,
and the sky scatters stars
across the garden
now stripped of flowers —
just like my life
without you here.

LINES

My love,

as once all roads led to Rome,
so all the lines in my palm
lead only to you.

FIGURINE

My love,

without you
I am nothing more
than a clay figurine,
not yet fired in the kiln
left in the rain.

Rustling

My love,

there is so much silence around
that I can hear silence rustling.

Engraving

My love,

I carved your name into my heart,
believing it would stay forever —
but time slipped softly through the day,
and quietly stole it far away.

ECLIPSE

My love,

a sky without sun
and without moon
might exist.
I, without you,
could not.

DEW

My love,

in the morning,
on blades of grass,
angels' tears
shine like diamonds,
and in their glow,
I hold your hand at last.

FLIGHT

My love,

I wish I were a bird,
free in the open sky,
with nothing to stop me
from reaching you.

SNOWTIME

My love,

perhaps I am in another place
than where I should be,
or in another time
than the one I know.
A time condensed into a moment,
as pure as white snow,
I would not wish to let it pass —
yet, willing or not, it will go.

PENDULUM

My love,

our hearts,
a perfect pendulum,
beat days and nights
into moments of love.

TRANSIENCE

My love,

tomorrow, today becomes yesterday.
No matter how I try to hold it still,
time slips it from my hands
and quietly steals it away.
Tomorrow, today will be yesterday.

GRAYSEASON

My love,

the nameless season begins.
Autumn light melts into shadows
and pours the world's sorrows into gray.

TRANSFORMATION

My love,

don't leave!
I will become a snowball,
so you can melt me
in the hollow of your palms;
a piece of clay,
so you can give me
any shape you want,
a grain of salt,
to give flavor to your life.

PROVIDENCE

My love,

nothing in this world is random.
Not even the fact that I always long for you.

MELANCHOLY

My love,

the sweet melancholy of years gone by
slowly turns into the despair
of moments never lived.

SPHERE OF NOTHINGNESS

My love,

I am like a dandelion fluff,
a sphere of nothingness
at the first drop of rain.

QUESTIONS

My love,

don't ask me why,
ask me no questions —
and if you do,
do not wait for any answer.
How could a fish ever know
how vast the sea is?

CLAY

My love,

without you I am nothing more
than a lump of clay
in the hands of an unskilled potter.

TIDE

My love,

the wave breaks on the shore
and withdraws.
Behind it remains only the waiting
for the next wave,
and in that quiet interval
I learn the measure of longing.

CALLING

My love,

if you only knew how my wings ache!
Sometimes I fear they might fall
as I fly toward you.
It pains me deeply,
but still I heed your call.

EMPTINESS

My love,

for some time now
I move in a hollow, foreign space.
Neither words nor silence,
have any meaning left,
nothing rings, nothing stays,
for without you,
nothing holds its place.

SECRETS

My love,

ask me nothing.
Women,
if they are true to themselves,
keep their secrets
buried deep within their soul,
and I will hold them safe and whole.

WORDSEED

My love,

each time I step into a word,
a world is born behind me,
as if, touched only by my dream,
words bear fruit with desperate haste,
for love has gently left its gleam.

BEFORE

My love,

sometimes I turn my thoughts back
to the time before we met
and try to imagine life without you.
Can you believe I never succeed?

PERHAPS

My love,

perhaps!
Perhaps the word itself may be divine:
the thought that one day
you may return to me,
that you might still remember our nights,
that for us, perhaps, a future yet may be.

DREAM

My love,

life is a dream
lived
as we dream it.

HORIZON

My love,

in the evening the sea rises
beneath my window,
and in the morning withdraws
until it meets the sky.
How is it that neither you nor I
can cross the distance between us?

You are always in my heart —
how come we remain forever apart?

SERPENT

My love,

every Paradise hides its serpent.
Without the lure of sin, empty of desire,
we would never know,
and never see,
how sweet the forbidden can be.

UMBRELLA

My love,

the sky, a giant umbrella,
cannot shield us from rain, from sun,
and, most of all, from ourselves.
Even beneath its vast dome
we are soaked, we are scorched.
Yet together, we face the storm.

AVALANCHE

My love,

I push toward you a mountain of words.
You push toward me a mountain of words.
Between us — silence.

OBLIVION

My love,

forgetfulness,
this beast of prey,
circles us
and every day
one memory
wraps itself in fog
and disappears.

OUTLINE

My love,

our outline comes from God.
To shade it into good or evil
is up to us alone.

FIRMAMENT

My love,

look at the vault of the sky,
how it is fastened to nothingness
with great diamond nails.
And we, pinned to the ground,
bellow —
unsure what to do,
and where to go,
as a terrible wind
begins to blow.

BLADE

My love,

the word is a double-edged sword,
drawn from its sheath.
Do not wound me, hoping it will pass!

BORDER

My love,

between you and me
there is no abyss, no mountain,
no sea to keep us apart.
Between you and me
are only a few words
spoken in anger, long ago —
between you and me now,
only a border of words. Unseen,
a trace that haunts the space between.

SHIP

My love,

I am a ship on a raging sea.
You, the shore of my desires —
the first and the last.

AFFINITY

My love,

I am bound to you
as gold to its gleam,
as salt to its taste,
as the bird to its wings,
and roots to a tree.
I am bound to you like destiny
that can never be changed.

CANE

My love,

I cling to you
like a blind man in the street
to his white cane.

STARS

My love,

how distant the day that was,
how close the night that comes —
so close I hear the stars ignite
and then go out again,
sky and all,
inside me,
silently.

SEAL

My love,

there are moments that stick to the soul
like a seal to wax,
imprinting the lines of a future
unknown, yet to unfold.

FRACTURE

My love,

before meeting you,
I didn't believe one could fall
more than once,
that one could break,
torn by pain,
piece by piece,
and still go on.

DAYBREAK

My love,

darkness is deepest
just before the day begins.

GRAYFOREST

My love,

a scale of grays,
subtly measured,
of a forest stripped of muses,
bare,
before the winter freezes it —
such is my soul now
that you have gone,
leaving me alone.

GHOSTS

My love,

what lies ahead no longer mirrors
what we left behind.
The present is already haunted
by ghosts.

VANISHING

My love,

how strange!
All things feel so distant,
and yet so near,
as if only yesterday.
Where, where have they gone?
Does all that rises… inevitably fall,
leaving nothing at all?
Does all that rises always have a sunset?

TWILIGHT

My love,

evening settles over the world —
over me, over dreams;
snow gathers upon my temples,
and my steps grow heavy —
leading nowhere.

LEAVES

My love,

have you ever heard
the terrifying sound
leaves make as they detach
and fall and fall and fall,
like a symphony
of things that sing
before they cease to be?

BLUEFOREST

My love,

my blue forests,
woven from dreams,
are now a procession of shadows —
wandering, lost,
and no one knows where to.

WINTERPATHS

My love,

memory gives birth to paths
we wander through the winter.
Now, when it is so cold,
I keep remembering the mornings
when your hands found me
before the light did.

FOAM

My love,

how was I to know
our love would last
no longer than the foam
of a wave touching the shore?

CONTINUITY

My love,

between the me of today
and the me of yesterday,
a virtual identity
resting on an illusory continuity,
like that between night and day,
between presence and absence.

FUTILITY

My love,

all words have been spoken.
All wrongs have been done.
All worlds have been invented.
Our hands kiss each other, frightened.

BELLS

My love,

when heaven fills with tolling bells,
only then, only then,
I, your mirror and your body,
may shatter into shards.
From a vessel with two handles,
only one will remain,
only then, only then,
when the earth shall be
nothing more than memory.

CHESTNUT

My love,

it rains,
and chestnut leaves,
palms with fingers
spread on sidewalk,
suddenly remind me
of your long-ago caresses.

RITUAL

My love,

do you not feel the ritual's futility?
No matter how often we repeat it,
it leaves behind mysterious passages,
beyond our reading.

VINE

My love,

in your absence,
my dreams sleep,
wrapped like a vine,
around a column.

BIRDS

My love,

how can I shelter my certainties,
so many scattered by cruel time,
like restless migratory birds
setting out toward the South?
How?

UNDERTOW

My love,

a wave of time swallowed us both,
dragging us into the sea of forgetting.

MEMORIES

My love,

with every passing day,
time brings silence closer —
however, this silence is not empty,
but full of memories.

DEFEAT

My love,

our love killed the time —
and time defeated our love.

GUARDIAN

My love,

take care of my love;
only it can protect you from evil,
just as cats in silent, ancient libraries,
eyes half-closed, unyielding,
guard old and rare books from the rats,
patient as time, faithful to the dark.

FRAME

My love,

my outline merged with yours:
two paintings in the same frame.

SWORD

My love,

did you not know
there are words sharper
than a samurai's sword?
Did you not know that words
can turn a life into hell,
or into heaven?

Rain

My love,

a melodic rain falls over my life
like a calling.
It is your voice
coming from afar.

Horse

My love,

when I will leave,
do not try to crucify me
on lines of ink,
nor color me pink.
I was what I was —
a white horse
painted for a moment on snow.
The snow melted, horse and all.

SOURCE

My love,

I know you will return.
After flooding everything in its path,
does water not long,
in the end,
to return to its bed?

CREASES

My love,

time has folded in on itself.
From its creases
flicker brief memories,
moments I feel I have lived
in other lives,
and for a few fleeting seconds,
I touch their miracle.

Song

My love,

I cannot live without you,
as birds cannot live
without their song.

Snails

My love,

giant snails have entered the city.
From fear, the gardens begin to ring
rustling bells of dry leaves.
Come, my love,
do not leave me
a prey to autumn.

IRONY

My love,

what an irony!
to set out in search of something new,
and yet carry forever with you
the weight of your past life.

SALT

My love,

like a *salinero*
bearing his basket of salt on his back,
I carry in my soul
all our memories,
both dark or bright,
woven together in endless light.

MIRROR

My love,

I lit the lamp
and suddenly we both appeared
in the room that had been full of darkness.
But when I looked in the mirror,
my loneliness had doubled.

PAST

My love,

once the future floated around me,
tempting as spring.
Now only the past circles me,
dressed in gray,
monotonous,
empty days.

PETALS

My love,

when you left me,
words fluttered from my lips
like fragile petals breaking free,
trembling with fear,
and carried by the wind
to a world I cannot steer.

INEVITABLE

My love,

I slammed the door behind me
and left, swearing never to return.
But where could I go
when every road
leads to you?

CUP

My love,

of all the women
who passed through your life,
I alone held in my hands
a cup from which we had drunk
a drop of happiness.

SPHINX

My love,

time has begun to flow differently,
like a system of mistranslated signs.
Even your face, once so familiar,
has grown as inscrutable
as the Sphinx of Memphis.
What is happening to the world, my love?
To you? To me?

ETERNITY

My love,

where might I rent
a parcel of infinity
to rest my weary soul?

SEASON

My love,

cold drops.
Summer weeps
for when it will return,
once more adorned
with fire red poppies
and blue cornflowers,
who knows if it will not be in vain,
if it will still find here
what it left behind again.

THOUGHT

My love,

I remain silent.
I do not dare to dress my thought
in its roughened bark.
How fragile is its core,
how endless its promise!
How treacherous, the word!

UNSPOKEN

My love,

unnoticed, time slipped away from us
those moments when we existed
only for one another.
The years came and went.
And so many things,
so many things, my love,
we never said.

ORBIT

My love,

each of us has an orbit
of our own, like a planet.
Only I entered yours.

ABYSS

My love,

I stand at the edge
of all I do not understand
and what I cannot grasp tears me apart —
the past is sometimes an enemy
that still attacks me,
and the future, a false friend
I have learned to fear.

DUSK

My love,

it is toward evening.
In vain we try to deceive ourselves.
The day's shadows withdraw softly.
Behind us rises a wall of fog;
ahead, no road —
only a thick, impenetrable wall of smoke.

UNBORN

My love,

I wish to sleep so deeply—
the sleep of the unborn, without dreams,
for I do not know what I was born for.
To live a moment,
only to return to silence once more?

SNOWFALL

My love,

it is snowing heavy flakes,
and the spirals of smoke above the houses
look like enormous life rings,
reminding me of your caring wings,
lifting me whenever I need you.

QUIET

My love,

nothing of what exists
is as it once appeared to be.
The world has changed so much,
has become so loud,
that only when I am with you,
I find my quiet and what is really true.

Biographical Note

Crisula Stefanescu is a Romanian poet, novelist, playwright, editor, and literary translator, whose work explores memory, exile, love, and the metaphysical dimensions of time. Her writing combines lyrical intensity with philosophical depth and has been published in Romania and abroad.

She graduated from the Faculty of Philology at the University of Bucharest in 1972. In 1982, she emigrated to Germany. From 1983 onward, she was affiliated with *Radio Free Europe*, initially as a research analyst at the *Radio Free Europe Research Institute* (1983–1992). During this period, she authored and published analytical and synthetic studies for the Western press, focusing on major events, ideological frameworks, and representative figures of Romanian cultural life.

In 1992, she joined the Broadcasting Department of Radio Free Europe, where she served as editor of the cultural program *Controversies Confluences East–West* until 1995, when the radio station relocated to Prague.

She currently resides with her husband, the writer Andi Stefanescu, in a Bavarian village near Munich.

Crisula Stefanescu is the author of approximately thirty published volumes, spanning poetry, drama, prose, essays, interviews, journals, and children's literature. *(www.crisulastefanescu.com)*

Poetry

- *The Spell of the Hour* (1998)

- *Signs* (1999)

- *The Gate of Kisses* (2004) — bilingual edition Romanian / English

- *The Departure of the Serpent* (2005)

- *Mr. Borges' Gift* (2010; revised and expanded edition, 2022)

- *Cliffs with Love* (2021)

- *The Kingdom of the Girls with Long Hair* (2021)

- *On the Wings of Time* (2023)

- *The Past Comes Raging Toward Me* (2024)

- *Chimeras* (2024)

Novels

- *Bonsai: The Story of the Fortunate Girl* (2022)

- *A Journey by Elevator: Chronicle of an Emigration* (with Monella Kaplan, epistolary novel, 2017)

Short Prose

- *Caprices* (2024)

Plays

- *Anna and Satan* (1999)

- *Cerberus and Deianira* (2017)

Journals

- *In Wonderland: Pages from an American Journal* (2022)

Children's Literature

- *Tutu. Uimitoarele aventuri ale motanului Tutu povestite de el insusi,* Sedcom Libris 2011, Aius 2023

- *Mitsou: Les aventures extraordinaires d'un chat végétalien.* L'Age d'Homme, Switzerland, 2014; French version of Țuțu, translated by Iulia Niculescu

- *TSUTSU, Les extraordinaries aventures d'un gatet vegetarià, explicades per ell mateix,* Universitat Rovira i Virgili, 2025. Catalan version of Țuțu, translated by Lilica Voicu-Brey

Interviews

Conversations and interviews with and about major European and Romanian intellectuals, including Alexandru Cioranescu, Augustin Buzura, Ioana & Sergiu Celibidache, Alexandr Zinoviev, Dan Er. Grigorescu-Negropontes.

- *Between Admiration and Love,* 2000, 2021

- *The Terror of Illusion*, Polirom, 2004

- *Sergiu & Ioana Celibidache: Secrets of a Great Love*, LangenMüller, Munich, 2011

- Dan Er. Grigorescu-Negropontes, *The Inner Exile,* Vremea, 2016

- *Value and Truth*, Aius, 2021

- *Alexander Zinoviev, a Man of Paradoxes,* Aius, 2022

- *Interviews on Radio Free Europe,* Aius, 2023

Translation & Editorial Work

Crisula Stefanescu translates contemporary Romanian poetry into English and has presented it in literary circles in Munich. She has translated and edited major bilingual volumes of Romanian poetry, including works by Ana Blandiana and Octavian Paler. She is also the editor of important archival and scholarly editions devoted to Romanian writers and intellectuals in exile.

Critical References

Many of the poems call to mind the *Rubaiyat* of Omar Khayyam. Formally, even if they do not follow the strict model, there is an evident tendency in Crisula Stefanescu's work to condense philosophical meaning into as few lines as possible, some poems having the extreme concentration of haiku. In terms of content, the resemblance is even stronger: the poet's verses are born of that diffuse anxiety before the fatality of time's passing, doubled by the implicit urge to live the moment. Her verses open gateways of reflection toward the great truths of life and, as with Omar Khayyam's *Rubaiyat*, the reader will remain thoughtful long after finishing the book."

Tudorel URIAN

"In my opinion, a poet must first be heard. If the poet remains only between the pages of a book and is not heard, something is missing—some essential sound in the diapason needed to impose itself on public consciousness. I have heard Crisula Stefanescu, and in her calm simplicity I have heard the sound of song."

Nicolae FLORESCU

"What struck me was the stylized ease with which she assumes her femininity. It was a poetry of sensuality, gladly shedding roughness, essentializing itself into striking images, into a calligraphy of taut contours."

Titu POPESCU

"Her poetry draws attention through the luminosity and morning freshness of the text, as well as through an ever-active artistic intelligence, thanks to which the reader is constantly surprised and invariably won over."

Alex STEFANESCU

"Crisula's poetry is the reconstruction of a shattered universe, from which memory has preserved in its depths only the terror of the storm that turned it into ruins. The themes are characteristic: sadness, fear, storm, absence, death, suffering—everything that casts a mist and darkness over the luminous beauty of life."

Alexandru CIORANESCU

"A wanderer in the universe of an intimate time, the poet Crisula Stefanescu intertwines in her lyrical creations—both confessional and revelatory—the meanders of love with the nostalgia of untainted sensitivity, building a poetics of re-calling, of re-uniting primordial unity."

Dana DAD

"What unsettled me from the very first moment in Crisula Stefanescu's verses was the strange coexistence of the lack of ostentation and the power to obsess."

Ana BLANDIANA

"For the author, the power to dream and the power to live do not seem distinct; both are vital necessities. The poet is a thinker, contemplative and in search of the oxygen of intelligence, and writing, which opens to her the mysterious gates of life—is, in the end, life itself."

Angela NACHE-MAMIER

"Verses ignited by acute, typically feminine sensuality... Crisula Stefanescu brings a lyrical discourse of marked, emphatically underlined originality, given by the frankness and total, impressive sincerity of her raw lyrical attitudes, uncensored by contrived, false modesties, by feminine strategies and tactics of seduction, secret and hidden, all guarded by an ever-awake lucidity."

Victor RUSU

"All the poems possess a familiarity that draws you in, that you recognize, that you have been or are a part of; insidiously, the verse seems to probe you, to challenge you to sustain it, to carry it further like your own cross."

George VULTURESCU

Contents